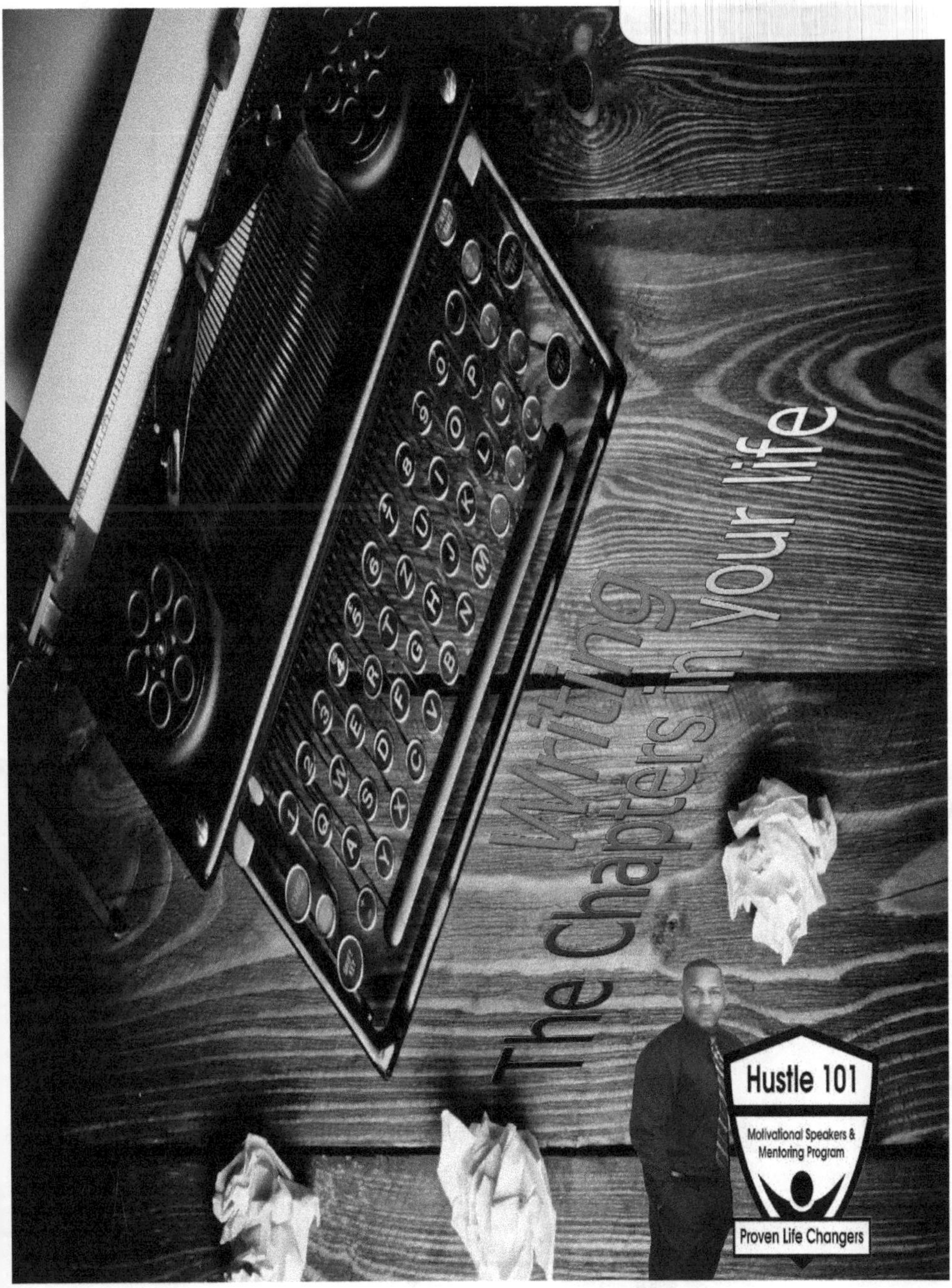
The Writing
Chapters in
your life
Hustle 101
Motivational Speakers & Mentoring Program
Proven Life Changers

Writing

(The chapters in your life)

Copyright © 2021 by **Santiego Rivers** & **Amanda Miller**

All rights reserved. This book may not be reproduced or transmitted in any form without the written permission of the authors.

"no copyright infringement is intended."

ISBN 978-1-7376037-6-4

Where you are currently at in your life does not have to be where you end up in your life. Your life is a novel filled with chapters.

How many chapters will be in your novel? That is a question that only you can answer. We get trapped reading or reliving the same chapter in our life, unwilling to turn the page and move on to a new beginning.

When it comes to your book, you are the author, editor, and illustrator. If you don't like something in your book, rewrite the story or improve your next chapter.

There is no need to be depressed about the past or anxious about the future. Instead, you must learn to live in the present and embrace all the chapters in your life.

The **"not so good"** moments in your life give the **"Great"** moments their joy.

This book will teach you how to turn the pages in your life and write the story of your life in a way that makes you happy with the outcome.

We all will sometimes struggle in our life. We will face adversity that will buckle us to our knees.

The strong ones know that when they face the type of adversity that puts them on their knees, only God puts them in a place where they will be their most prevailing.

I had always stood my tallest when I was on my knees praying.

My strength has always come from my **faith** and ability to **work hard**. I know that my father would never bring me across the mountains and deserts that I have traveled to leave me in the valley of woe.

Nothing happens in our life that God has not ordained that we will not be strong enough to overcome despite our ability to put ourselves in situations that do not benefit us.

I have had moments in my life that made me contemplate taking my own life. There are pieces of those feelings that still exist within me today, but my faith keeps me from going down that corridor.

We all have corridors in our life that serve us no purpose but to keep us from our purpose in life.

When we travel down those passages, we encounter the obstacles that make it hard for us to return to the path we were meant to travel.

From dark passages to bad chapters in our lives, we will deal with all the unfortunate choices we make one day. Embrace those moments in life. Those choices will become the chapters in our lives meant to show us how we overcame those setbacks and kept moving forward.

Unfortunately, many of us get stuck in the wrong chapters in our life, unwilling to write the next chapter in our story.

We are the authors who write the stories that we have encountered. I have faced demons and monsters in my life, but I have never met them alone.

There are chapters from my juvenile years that followed me into my adult years. But, unfortunately, the child in me was unwilling to give the adult the pen to write the new chapters in my life.

Facing trauma in our life at an early age makes us fear moving on to a new chapter because fear can make cowards of the strongest people when you must face it at an early age in life.

Many of us can recall all the trauma that we have encountered in our life quicker than we can remember moments that we were happy or how we overcame an awful experience.

Why does our mind work like this? In my opinion, the adversity that we faced in our life, which was supposed to teach us how to overcome it, and our strength and ability to stand tall only left us feeling defeated and unsure about ourselves.

We were supposed to take all the trials and tribulations that we faced in life as an opportunity to grow. Those obstacles were never meant to defeat us!

Facing those roadblocks allowed doubt and fear to creep into our minds, which paused our pen from writing beyond that point.

We deposited negative thoughts in our mind to the point where when we face adversity in the future; we revisit those moments when we encountered a similar obstacle and remembered how we responded to those situations in the past.

Reliving negative past experiences hoping to get a positive outcome is wrong. We are wrong to do this on so many levels.

We become so accustomed to how we handled things in our past that we allow our past to dictate our future.

If we don't want people holding us to our past, we must stop holding ourselves to our past mistakes.

Don't be ashamed of anything that happened in your past. On the contrary, it would be best to make peace with your past indiscretions and learn from them so that the memories you recall are about how you overcame obstacles and not how the barriers you faced became your roadblock in life.

How does that old saying go?

"When life gives you lemons, you make lemonade."

I don't know about you, but I like lemonade. It takes a lot of lemons to make lemonade, so you must be willing to take all the lemons that life gives you and put them to use in a way that benefits you.

Each day we must make positive mental deposits in our mind that allows us to use them when we need them.

The more positive thoughts that we deposit, the easier it becomes to withdraw from positive memories from our past experiences.

The mind is a powerful tool! Therefore, you must decide how you will use your mind for the betterment of your life.

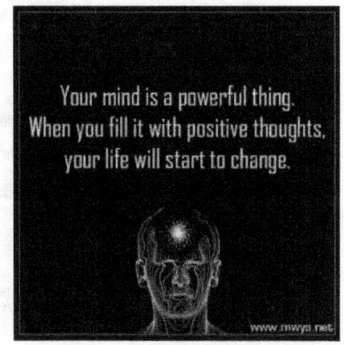

Your life can be beautiful if you allow it to be! Therefore, only you can decide what your book will be about when it is complete.

Don't sweat the small stuff in your life. Sometimes certain things in your life must fall apart for everything to come together the way it should.

My life has been shattered to pieces a thousand times over, but from past experiences, I know that they have all made me a better person.

I survived all the past storms in my life, which makes me sure of one thing. I am a survivor!

Life doesn't get easier! Instead, we get stronger to face and overcome all the obstacles that life will present us.

Life will challenge you in more ways than one!

Either you can complain or learn to change/adapt to all the challenges life brings your way.

I fully understand that we are all one struggle away from our breaking point, but we are also even closer to success if we continue to fight.

Your success will inspire those who desperately need to be inspired. There's somebody out there that needs to hear your story.

Your story can lead to a transformation in their life.

What will you do with your pen?

It took years for me to understand how the worst chapters became the best chapters in my life.

Character, determination, and the will to **survive** are forged in the valley, not on any mountain tops.

I had to get to the point in my life where I was sick and tired of being sick and tired to do something positive to change my life for the better.

When you are standing on the mountain top, you may find it hard to remember what it took to get there in your life.

On the mountain top, most people forget about the sacrifices that they had to make to reach the peak and survive the valley.

I keep a token that I brought from the valley that I use for inspiration to remind me that my path to the top of the mountain was paved with many sacrifices, tears, hard work, and losses that I can never get back.

To get the things you want in life, you must be willing to lose some things you don't want to live without in your life.

Being **successful** is not easy or **comfortable**. Those two words will never go together to make sense. If you ever see those two words together, it is because someone like me is trying to get you to understand that you can only have one of those things in your life at a time.

Learning to understand the difference between being comfortable and **successful** was one of the longest and hardest chapters that I had to live in my life.

It is like a child learning that you can't be considered or treated like an adult living in your parents' home, and they are still taking care of you. But, unfortunately, the sad reality is that adults take care of themselves.

Another chapter that took me a long time to move on from was dealing with losing someone from my life that I was not ready to let go of physically. However, I still hold onto the memories and lessons they taught me over the years we spent together.

I have written a few books about learning to let go and accept things that my heart and mind will genuinely never comprehend.

I will let my friend Amanda Miller tell you about her experience and why she decided to bring her pen to paper and share an essential chapter in her life with you.

Sometimes, it takes hearing the same story from a different person to realize or get the message that we need to understand to make sense of what we are going through in our lives.

Introducing (Author) **Amanda Miller**

My name is Amanda Miller, and the following reasons are why I bring my pen to my paper, writing the chapters in my life.

I lost my mom at a young age. It has affected me majorly. Every time I see someone get a hug, talk, or even tell their mom they love them, it makes me jealous.

I always think to myself about why I lost my mom at such a young age? It makes no sense to me in my mind. Yet, there is never a day that I don't think about my mom.

She was my best friend; she was someone I could talk to, and she supported me no matter what I did in my life. For me, it is so much harder without her in my life.

My dad, well, doesn't always know the answer to girl problems. If I had one more chance to see her, I would be so happy. I miss her voice, smell, and her touch. You don't realize how much you appreciate someone until they're gone.

Death is one of the hardest things to look past in my mind. But, I always try to think happy thoughts and remember that other people have/or are dealing with a similar situation like mine. I am not alone, and yes, it is okay to cry still. But, the pain of losing my mom will never be gone. So please, tell your mom or dad or just anyone you have that you love them will they are still present in your life. You never know when it is their last breath.

"If there ever comes a day when we can't be together, keep me in your heart, I'll stay there forever."
- Winnie the Pooh

The other reason that I brought my pen to my paper was that I felt insecure and like I was being judged on how "pretty" I was.

Those comments from other people made me put on makeup and try to change my appearance. I tried to hide my natural beauty to be "accepted." But that is not me. I want to feel like me and feel like I am don't have to impress other people. So, I must be happy being myself, which is often hard for people my age.

I can't feel imprisoned or trapped by other peoples' opinions of me. It took some time, but I finally learned to embrace my inner beauty. I barely wear makeup anymore, and I feel freer. I'm happier than ever was when I learned to leave that chapter in my life and start a new one.

I finally feel like me, and I'm not pretending to be someone who I'm not. Starting a new chapter in my life allowed me to embrace my true self and be me!

It took me some time but, I finally learned that I am beautiful no matter what!

The last reason that I put my pen to my paper writing my new chapter in life is because I want to remember how far I have come and how far I will be heading when I turn the pages and start the next chapter in my life. We must continue living and don't take things for granted. We're all in this together as we become the authors of our own story!

(Author) Amanda Miller

I say the following respectfully, but in a way, that hopefully will inspire you to make the needed change in your life:

"No one cares about the fact that you are going through a tough time in your life!"

Put your grown people undergarments on and make the needed changes in your life to get the outcome that you desire!

When it comes to my life today, the people who see me now don't know or care about the struggles that I went through to get to this point where I am claiming victory!

The people who love the smile that I wear on my face today don't know or care about the years of pain and struggles it took for me to have something to smile about finally!

I don't come from comfortable beginnings!

I had to work for everything that I got in life. However, the most challenging obstacle I had to overcome was thinking that I was entitled to my success and happiness.

If the current chapter in your life is a living hell for you, then why would you choose to stay there when you have the pen in your hand?

Allow me to put it in another way for you:

If you are going through hell, why stop there?

Don't put a question mark where God put a period to your struggle and pain in life. Life is filled with seasons, so don't get stuck in the winter, not preparing for the spring, summer, and fall.

When those different seasons come in your life, you will still be dressed in your winter clothes, wondering why you are miserable.

It would help if you left the snow and the cool weather in the winter and prepared for the current season in your life.

The same concept must occur when you decide to write a new chapter in your life story.

Be the change that you need in your life to make it better for you.

"The world or the people in it doesn't owe us anything!"

We owe it to ourselves to live the life that we want and find happiness here on earth.

Reclaim your life! Discover and hold on to your joy!

Success, happiness, and **joy** is not an overnight journey. So, you need to pack a lunch and be prepared to put in some hard work to achieve anything in life worth achieving.

It doesn't take anything to achieve failure. The only thing you need to do to reach failure in your life is to keep doing the same thing that you are currently doing in your life.

If what you are currently doing in your life was working for you, you would already have **success, happiness**, and **joy** in your life.

If you live on earth, you will never be finished writing the chapters in your life.

I am up to thirty books, and I am only at the beginning of writing about my journey to where I am going in my life.

The only thing that holds you back in life or that will allow you to move forward in your life is your mind.

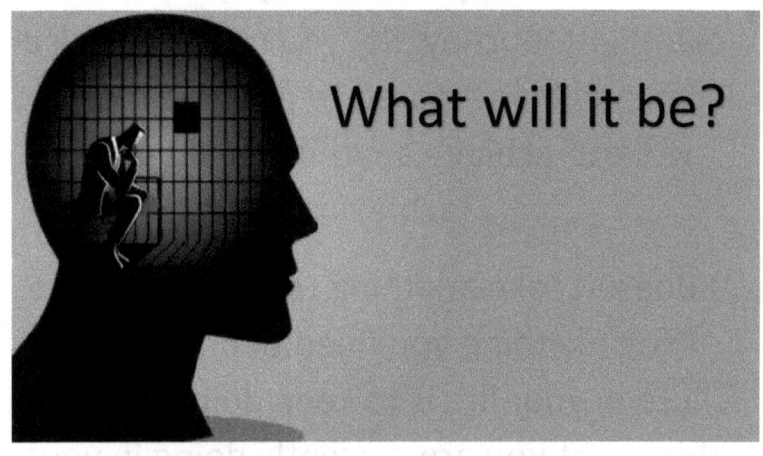

How long will you allow yourself to be a prisoner of your mind before you decide to grab the pen and write the next chapter in your life?

What will you declare...?

This book is dedicated to all the dreamers who decided to become the Authors of their stories!

www.ingramcontent.com/pod-product-compliance
Lightning Source LLC
Chambersburg PA
CBHW071015160426
43193CB00012B/2057